Ancient Amerindian Symbols
With
Old World Connections

/ | \

By
Jim Michael
Ancient Kentucke Historian
President of the Ancient Kentucke Historical Association

Final Edit
Marilyn Michael
Secretary Ancient Kentucke Historical Association

Jim Michael
1324 Garden Hill Place
Louisville KY 40245
MARMAKHA@hotmail.com

Order this book online at www.trafford.com
or email orders@trafford.com

Most Trafford titles are also available at major online book retailers.

Printed in Victoria, BC, Canada.

ISBN: 978-1-4251-1159-5 (sc)

*Our mission is to efficiently provide the world's finest, most comprehensive book publishing
service, enabling every author to experience success. To find out how to publish your
book, your way, and have it available worldwide, visit us online at www.trafford.com*

Trafford rev. 2/23/2010

 www.trafford.com

North America & international
toll-free: 1 888 232 4444 (USA & Canada)
phone: 250 383 6864 ♦ fax: 812 355 4082

Ancient Amerindian Symbols With Old World Connections

/ / \

56 Pictures /|\

/ | \

Dedication

This book is dedicated to the thousands of Christian men, women, and children who left their homeland in Britannia in the mid-sixth century in seven hundred boats. They took everything they owned, including their animals, expecting never to return to their homeland again. They were promised a land rich and plentiful with plantable soil for farming. Their land had been devastated by a celestial atmospheric explosion which had created a vast wasteland around AD 562. They were led by their new king, Arthur II, and his brother Mathew [in British/Khumric he was known as Prince Madoc].

Prince Madoc had been blown into the Sargasso Sea by the waves and wind caused by the atmospheric comet explosion. He did not return to Britannia for ten years. The Brits sailed westerly in the direction of their ancients, which had been verified by their British Admiral Gwenon, as they were unsure of Madoc's star maps. They overcame their fear of falling into the abyss [the pit from which there is no return].

The seven hundred boats landed all over the shores of the American continent in AD 574. Then the newcomers explored the rivers and interior of America. They left their writings up the Missouri River to what is now Davenport, Iowa and up the Ohio River to what is now Pittsburg, Pennsylvania. This spiritual group brought with them a new form of Christianity which had many old-world symbols. [#1]

An evil blow fell on them when their 69-year-old king was killed by a volley of arrows. They mummified Arthur II, fitted him with a golden face mask, and nine men transported him back to Britannia in a bag inside a box. Although later their army was called home to protect the next kingship [Madoc's son Morgan], the footprint that they left can still be seen in the religious symbols of the Amerindians today.

#1. Michael, *Ancient Kentucke Inscriptions*, Chicago Spectrum Press. 2004.

/|\

Ancient Amerindian Symbols
With
Old World Connections

/ | \

Chapter One

Ancient Kentucke Historical Association

For 20 years now, the Ancient Kentucke Historical Association has been researching who was on this continent prior to Columbus other than the Amerindians. This entire area of research is very unpopular with almost all mainstream archaeologists. Since no other organized group is really involved in this research and all those who could be are fearful of stepping into the trap of loosing their standing in the academic community, our 70-member organization has attempted to fill this void.

In our first book, *Ancient Kentucke Inscriptions, Prince Madoc: Fact or Fiction,*[# 1.] we presented five proofs that the ancient British were here in the sixth century. According to Dr. Donald Jansen, [# 2] retired Kentucky professor of Archaeology, there are three acceptable proofs by the mainstream archaeologists. They are:

1. **Empiric.**
2. **Logical.**
3. **Speculative.**

Empiric is that proof that can be duplicated in any laboratory. This is like carbon dating and DNA. After you have established the empiric proof, then you can look for the logical evidence which fits. This would be oral traditions and historical evidence. Speculative proof is the easiest to dispute by other scholars if not supported by the first two. This would be like the speculations in the 1800s that the mounds and forts found in the Ohio Valley were just like the mounds and forts found in Britain from King Arthur's day. When you couple this with 20 to 30 published reports of encounters with Welsh-speaking Indians, it all seems to fit together.

This could be easily disputed by the scholars of the day by saying "No European was here before Columbus" or as a local anthropology professor would say, "There is not one shred of archaeological evidence to support anyone being here other than the Amerindians." Our findings are, of course, to the contrary.

The five proofs that we presented in *Ancient Kentucke Inscriptions, Prince Madoc: Fact or Fiction* to prove sixth century British presence are:

1. **American skeletal remains carbon dated to the seventh century with DNA to the British Isles.**
2. **Many sixth-century documents from the abbeys of the British Isles telling of the voyages.**
3. **Sixty translated messages from the American continent in the British alphabet.**

4. Ancient British mummies - one with an inscription.
5. Amerindian symbols with old world connections.

This brings us to the tenth chapter of the book *Ancient Kentucke Inscriptions, Prince Madoc: Fact or Fiction* which needs to be expanded into this book for more complete understanding.

FIG. 1   FIG. 2   FIG. 3

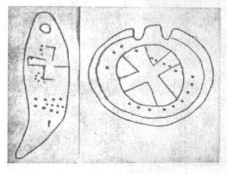

FIG. 4   FIG. 5

FIG. 55. MALTESE CROSS DECORATIONS.
Bear's teeth and gorget from Fox Field.

William Webb's findings

William Webb, the first head of the Archaeology department of the University of Kentucky, found the above symbols on a bear's tooth and a composite stone in Augusta, Kentucky. The circle-cross is obvious but the dotted turkey track on the bear's tooth is the most important symbol. If we had found this, it would be of little consequence but because an archaeologist found it, it becomes of great significance. The area where it was found is also very important because of all the British symbols that were found there.

/ | \

The above is our first symbol to be discussed. It was called a "turkey track" by American scholars. The symbol appears in petroglyphs and inscriptions as a solstice marker. In 1989, Jim Michael learned from Alan Wilson and Baram Blackett that this was an ancient religious symbol still used by the English government.

It is called an Awen sign and dates back to the time of Enoch. It has been explained as the light shining through the clouds and was accepted by these early people as the deity sign of Yahweh. According to Strabo, Caesars' historian in 51 B.C., the Bards following Moses' second commandment were not allowed to speak the Lord's name. They drew an Awen sign when they came to the Lord's name. The second level of Bards was called Ovates and they were permitted to use the name of God, Yahweh, with each other but were required to draw the Awen for any other use. The top level was the Druids, the Rabbis of the Lost Ten Tribes, and they could use the name of Yahweh openly.

In the 1400's, the Anglo-Saxon English government adopted the Awen from the British-Welsh as an official symbol, but we doubt if today they even know its origin or real meaning. Today it appears on many weapons of the English, on church pews and even prisoner's jackets. The most significant and important finding is that it is all over the American continent.

On page #3, you will see an example of the Awen sign on the bear's tooth, in dots, just as seen on the whorls from Troy. The largest Awen may be in the middle of the circle at the Newark Earthwork in Ohio and is over 100 feet from tip to tip. A computer animation appears on this page and the Awen can still be seen on the golf course which has a lease on this part of the structure until the year 2070. The Awen may give us the signature of the creators of the earthwork at Newark.

This brings us to one of the important philosophies of archaeology and anthropology — diffusion verses independent invention. Diffusion is like Christianity starting in one place and spreading throughout the world. Independent invention is what all the scholars say happened. People on two different continents, separated from each other, develop things independently. Thus, if left alone, they would all build pyramids and develop the same symbols etc. We find this a little hard to believe inasmuch as these symbols have old world connections.

As we enter the 21st century, we see the philosophy of individual invention starting to crumble. The mainstream archeologists can no longer disregard, as they have in the past, the new technology which is pointing to possibilities of ancient ocean travel. The time-honored chronology of no humans on this continent before the ice age corridor opened 10,000 to 13,000 years ago is no longer set in stone. The Clovis-first premise falls with the possibility of the French Solutrean point being the ancient predecessor and posing the possibility of the boat crossing.

Fifty-thousand-year-old tools found in South America and sculls of individuals identical to those of the people who reached Hawaii, Easter Island and Tahiti 50,000 to 60,000 years ago shatter the traditional idea that the only way to reach America was by foot. There was no land bridge to any of the Pacific islands yet they were peopled 50,000 to 60,000 years ago.

The 9,300 year old Kennewick Man is a good example of the evidence which points to the possibility of ocean travel prior to the ice corridor opening. His skull proved not to be Native American although no DNA has been done to date.

What is even harder to deny is that the 70,000-plus DNA cultures, now at Brigham Young University, taken from the full-blooded American Indians show the presence of the haplogene (or haplogroup X) which is European. The Native American DNA which can be traced back through the Bering Straits to Asia and Siberia carried only the haplogene A, B, C, and D.

Our findings that the ancient British came here at least in the sixth century become harder to deny as time goes on. And, as time goes on, the Ancient Kentucke Historical Association will produce additional DNA findings that will cement the sixth-century presence of the ancient Brits all over this continent. We know by the presence of their now-dead Coelbren alphabet with an ancient pedigree that they went at least up the Missouri River to Davenport, Iowa and up the Ohio River to Pittsburg, Pennsylvania. The Coelbren alphabet was the alphabet of the Welsh-speaking Indians and today we have at least 60 translated messages from the bedrock of this continent. The North American continent is the only continent on earth where carved epigraphics are not considered empiric proof, but we hope to change this through our research as time goes on. We will present more information on the Coelbren alphabet later in this book as it has a very ancient pedigree.

In order to understand the ancient activity in the Middle American continent, let us look at what we learned about this area from our first American military men and settlers. The name of Kentucke gives us some important clues as well as the oral traditions of the Native Americans.

By now, the reader is probably asking why we have spelled Kentucke with an "e" rather than Kentucky as it is now spelled. Kentucke or Kentucky is an

Amerindian name with several meanings which define what this territory was like in ancient times.

General George Rogers Clark

General George Rogers Clark met with a group of early settlers and military men before Kentucky became a commonwealth in 1792 and said that it should be spelled Kentucke. He told this group that Chief Tobacco told him that in Piankashaw it means "river of blood." He also mentioned that Chief Cornstalk told him that in Shawnee it means "dark and bloody ground." Then he related what Major Amos, the commander of the fort in Saint Louis, told him. Amos told him that a one-hundred-year-old Shawnee told him that "no one would ever want to live in Kentucke because of the souls of the many who were murdered there."

This not only defines what the Kentucke land was like but tells us that the Shawnee believed in the soul and that it left the body. There are those that think that no one actually lived in Kentucke, rather just hunted there. If no one lived in this area, why are there so many forts or ceremonial places, as they are called by today's archaeologists, up and down the Ohio River? It is well known that every year there was a migration of buffalo through Kentucke and they left a trail of their migration called the Buffalo Trace. The Warrior's Path was named for those who pursued them.

Artist and author George Catlin, in his map of mid-America, leaves us another important clue as to what was going on concerning this.

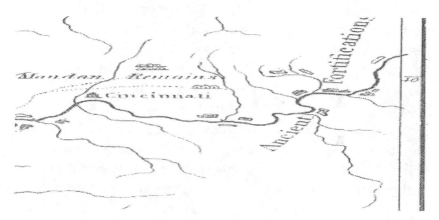

Ancient Fortifications – George Catlin

Catlin's map lists an ancient fortification blocking the approach to Kentucke. This fortification blocks movement either up or down the Ohio River. This stone wall can still be found on both sides of the river in

Portsmouth, Ohio. The wall is miles long and runs perpendicular to the Ohio River. This all fits with the oral traditions of a Native American race that would come down the river from the north and kill anyone who was living or hunting on their hunting ground. Mainstream archaeologists today do not feel that there are any fortifications on this continent and that all the earthworks are ceremonial including Fort Ancient. This is of course the current philosophy which is applied to the Amerindians not building forts and to the denial of ancient British contact.

In the audience with General George Rogers Clark was John Filson. Filson's name was later used on the title of the Louisville Historical Organization, now called the Filson Club. Filson is called by some "Kentucky's first historian." He could better be called Kentucky's first realtor. He did publish a 1784 book. The cover is seen here on page #12. It grades the Kentucky land into categories and gives a map of the proposed state of Kentucky. Note that Kentucke is spelled with an "e" and the book has a picture of Daniel Boone (1734–1820) leading new settlers into Kentucky.

It does make it look easy to come to Kentucky but we doubt if Boone wore a felt hat and a coat with a velvet collar. The book did make the frontiersman and pathfinder famous but fails to mention that Boone was captured and remained a prisoner for over a year in the Ohio area prior to his escape. Later he was commissioned by President Jefferson to widen the Buffalo Trace into a wagon trail. It might be important to note that he did, but rather than going to a major city in Kentucky, the trail went to the Ohio River at Augusta, Kentucky, across the Ohio River from Portsmouth, Ohio.

The location of where the Buffalo Trace leads is important to our story because many of the early symbols were found there by William Webb, the first head of the Archaeology Department at the University of Kentucky. While this two-wheel trail does not lead the newcomers to a major city in Kentucky, it does lead them to the Ohio River which was the main means of transportation to the ancients. It also leads us to the ancient fortifications which blocked the Buffalo Trace from the invaders from the north, further defining Kentucky.

Daniel Boone's 1818 Portrait
[Now hanging in the Filson Club in Louisville, Kentucky, painted two years prior to his death.]

John Filson's Book Kentucke [#2]

Note Daniel Boone leading newcomers through the Cumberland Gap with felt hat and the appearance of a velvet collar. Also note the man waving.

Boone's Oil Painting

It may not have been as peaceful as the artist makes it look. This picture is hanging in a tavern in Richmond, Kentucky. The collar may be a shadow on the book cover. The man waving has a whip or a sword.

Chapter One

#1. Michael, *Ancient Kentucke Inscriptions, Prince Madoc Fact or Fiction*, 2004.

#2. Filson, *the Discovery, Settlement and present State of Kentucke*, 1784.

Chapter Two

Constantine Rafinesque

Rafinesque should really be called the first historian of Kentucky. He was a professor of Natural History and Botany at Transylvania College in Lexington, Kentucky. Transylvania College was the first university west of the Allegheny Mountains. Later the medical department was moved to the University of Kentucky. He spent ten years there and recorded many of the anomalies found in Kentucky. Rafinesque's picture appears on the next page.

The sketch of Fawn Hoof was incorrectly published in the first edition of *Ancient Kentucke Inscriptions*. [#1] The correct sketch is presented at the end of this chapter.

In 1824, he published a book on the Antiquities of Kentucky. In this book, he stated that there was a large inscription on the Kentucky River but didn't say where. We searched the Kentucky River from its mouth at the Ohio River for around 100 miles down to Winchester. In 2004, three of our members called an inscription to my attention. It was large, just as Rafinesque had recorded, and was sent to Wilson and Blackett for translation. It had Coelbren letters and numbers along with Awen signs and tells that it is a solstice marker.

The Coelbren alphabet has a very old pedigree and may have been brought out of the Mesopotamian area with Abraham along with the all-seeing eye of God and the chevrons. We have reason to believe that the inscription found in Lot's cave was Coelbren rather than Greek as some scholars thought but could not translate. We now know that it was on the copper portions of the

Dead Sea Scrolls.   This inscription, found on four-pennyweight copper as seen on page #16 & 17, is Coelbren and is translated on page 515 of the *King Arthur Conspiracy*. [#2]

A Young Constantine Rafinesque

The translation has nothing to do with buried treasure and those who thought they could translate it have found no existing treasure. It, as you can see, is the earliest writing of the Exodus. Flavius Josephus talks about the copper tablets replacing the gold tablets which were stolen by the Egyptian Pharaoh Shishack or Tuthmosis III and taken to Egypt after the fall of the temple. Yes, they were hidden in the cave with the other Dead Sea Scrolls, but put there for safety rather than to preserve the secret hiding places.

Johns Hopkins University has been struggling with trying to translate this without knowing anything about Coelbren. When we contacted them in 1991 and told them that it was Coelbren and that we could translate it if they would provide us with pictures, they refused to believe us. They were receiving $40,000 a year to translate it and did not want anyone else involved. We told them that we did not want money, just recognition. [#3]

Jim Michael holding a copy of the Copper Portions of the Dead Sea Scrolls

A Close-up of the Copper Scrolls

[We were able to obtain these pictures from *Popular Mechanics*]

The scrolls had been rolled up and had to be carefully cut to straighten them out for translating. Johns Hopkins still thinks to this day that the letters are Greek with some code letters that they don't understand. They wrote that they were going to translate them in Greek, paying no attention to the fact that we told them they were Coelbren. [#3]

One of the problems that we all had in understanding this alphabet was that the ancients used combination letters and even hieroglyphs in their writings.

Because the ten tribes kept to themselves and migrated across Europe, their alphabet became obscure and, although it is right there where they left it, no one really took the time to connect it up and fill in the dots. The Phrygian, Etruscan, Rhaetian and the British Coelbren are all the same with very few differences. Wilson and Blackett were able to trace their ancestry back by following the Coelbren alphabet. We now think that the Coelbren alphabet may have come from Ur with Abraham and was borrowed by the Phoenicians and the Greeks. Julius Caesar wrote that the Brits had an alphabet and that it looked very much like the Greek alphabet. Two centuries later a Roman Catholic saint, Armianas Marcilinus, wrote that the Brits have an alphabet that looks like the Greeks' and the Greeks got their alphabet from the Brits.

Saint Justin, who wrote perhaps the best bible, explained that the difficulty that he had in translating into Latin both the original Hebrew versions of Matthew's Gospel and the earliest Luke Gospels was because they were written in Chaldaic language but used Hebrew letters. [#4]

This leaves Ancient Kentucke to wonder if in fact these were both using the Khumric language and the Coelbren alphabet. It amazes us to see how so much history is glossed over and how the Ten Tribes were hidden in plain sight by all of the important and knowledgeable men of their day. We now know that their alphabet was one of the earliest alphabets of all the early Semitic-speaking and writing peoples.

Since their Khumric language was in fact Chaldee, Abraham very well could have brought it from Ur. Thus both Luke and Matthew could have been speaking and writing Khumric and Coelbren.

18

Rafinesque's 1824 Inscription on Ky. River

In France, the Coelbren alphabet is called Iberian and Rafinesque might have seen it but this was not his area of expertise. He did recognize that there was an alphabet and that there were inscriptions here in Kentucky which he reported in his 1824 book. It may have looked a bit different to him because the writing on stone walls has much straighter strokes and the writing on metal and small tablets is more precise. [#5]

We now know that this inscription is written in Coelbren with Coelbren letters and numbers. The Awen can easily be seen in the top of the upper right hand corner. Wilson and Blackett will have the entire translation in their next book. The translation does tell how to use this inscription to tell the Solstice. This information was important to these early settlers to tell them the best time for planting and harvesting.

Rafinesque's Inscription Worked up

Each of these pictures is only about two thirds of the actual stone. The stone is so close to the river's edge that you must stand in the river or on a boat to see the whole inscription. This is, without doubt, one of the largest inscriptions on the continent. This brings our total of North American inscriptions to over 60 and most all of the translations can be seen in the *King Arthur Conspiracy*. All of the inscriptions have vowels and translate the same way. Some are on movable stones and others are on large stones and in shelters. Many have Awen symbols just as you can see in the inscription above. These translations are just one of the five proofs of the ancient British presence. [#2] [An actual translation of this inscription will be in Blackett and Wilson's next book.]

20

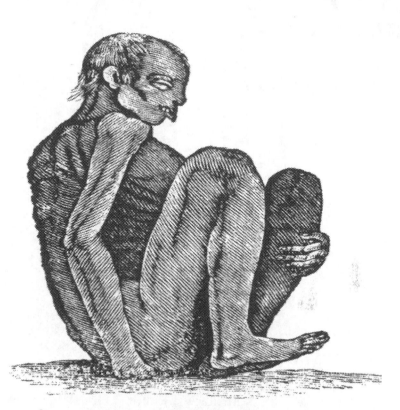

Rafinesque's Sketch of Fawn Hoof
[The incorrect sketch appears in *Ancient Kentucke Inscriptions*] [#1]

Chapter Two

1. Michael, *Ancient Kentucke Inscriptions*, Chicago Spectrum Press, 2004.
2. Berkley, *The King Arthur Conspiracy*, Trafford Press, Canada, 2005.
3. Shanks, *The Dead Sea Scrolls Forty Years Later*, Biblical Archaeological Society, 1991.
4. Busby, *The Bible Fraud*, The Pacific Blue Book Inc. 2001.
5. Rafinesque, *Ancient History, or Annals of Kentucky*, Frankfort, 1824.

Chapter Three

The Walam Olam

Delaware Hieroglyphics on Song Sticks

In 1820, a Kentucky doctor, Dr. Ward, was summoned to the White Water region of Indiana where a tribe of Delaware Indians was dying of white man's diseases. Most likely it was smallpox. A Native American who called himself a king asked him if he could give him some secret information. The tribal recipient of the information was already dead and the king did not know what to do.

Doctor Ward agreed and received 148 sticks with hieroglyphs on them. The king told him that it was the Walam Olam and Lene Lanape. One stick had the story of a great flood and another had the creation of mankind. Each of the sticks had a song which went along with the stick and the rest were the history of kings and what they did during their reign.

Today, the state archaeologist of Indiana places the Delaware tribe where Indianapolis is as seen on this map.

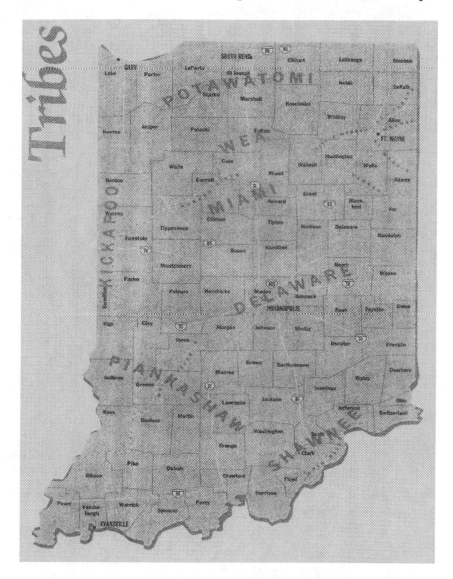

Native American Tribes of Indiana

Eli Lilly

Doctor Ward took the prayer or song sticks back to Kentucky and gave them to his friend Constantine Rafinesque. Rafinesque contacted the president of the Indiana Historical Society [Eli Lilly], the grandfather of the Eli Lilly seen above who started the pharmaceutical company, and they agreed to meet with several remaining members of the Delaware tribe to learn more about the strange sticks.

The two met with several members and asked them what the sticks were. Again the words were Walam Olam and Lene Lanape which Lilly wrote down. He felt that Walam Olam meant Red Score and that Lene Lanape was the ancient tribe perhaps like the Anasazi. The tribal members sang the songs which accompanied the sticks.

If Lilly had written down Gwalam Olam, it would have meant "organization of every man." Lene Lanape spelled the same means "secret or veiled knowledge" or "scholarship" in the Khumric-Welsh. This error has created a tribe by this name for which there are no members or DNA. Twenty years later Lilly published the Walam Olam and gave every member of his historical society a copy. [#1]

The question is "what is the origin of recording history on sticks?" It goes back to biblical times and to Ezekiel who wrote in Ezekiel XXXVIII 16–20: "Son of Man take thee one stick and write upon it for Judah and for the sons of Israel and his companions: then take another stick and write upon it for Joseph" etc. Then again in Numbers: "Take every one of you a rod and write your name on your rod." This is accountability and the ancient British Bards and Druids were following this doctrine to the letter. The Bards [historians] went from town to town with triangular sticks, which fit into an elucidator, recording the births of the illustrious. After returning to the abbeys, the sticks were recopied onto velum or parchment as seen on the next pages.

On certain important occasions, the Bards would take the sticks out of the abbeys and sing the songs that went with each stick. Believe it or not, every one of us has sung some of these songs to our children, one of which is about a king and what he did. This tradition will continue for generations to come. Old King Cole is just one of these songs. It is really about King Coel who lived in Britain several hundred years before Christ.

The point of this is that this system of writing on song sticks in the same language and meaning on two different continents flies in the face of the scholars and archaeologists who say that everything on this continent was "independently invented."

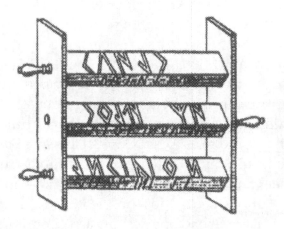

The Elucidator was a frame composed of a number of sticks, some 3 sided, others squared, on the flat surface of which were carved the Bardic aphorisms. The 3 sided ones contained a complete triad; the 4 sided ones a stanza (See Ezekiel xxxvii 16.)

Elucidator

This is an example of one of the ancient elucidators that was used to carry and store the sticks used to record the names of all the important kings and their offspring. Note the Coelbren letters on the sticks. These are the sticks that were later taken out of the abbeys and sung to the public gatherings on important occasions. [#2]

After the information was gathered by the bards [historians], it was taken back to the abbeys and rerecorded on velum for permanent keeping as seen here.

Bards and Monks Recording in the Abbey

The question has been raised as to the whereabouts of the Walam Olam song sticks? When Rafinesque was fired by the president of Transylvania College, all of his personal things were placed outside of his locked room. Rafinesque had very little money and received only board and room and had to vacate the premises with all his belongings. [There is a receipt for candles that he had used for lighting in his dorm room.]

Some say that the president was unhappy with the fact that Rafinesque was not in his classroom but out in the field with most of his class. Others say that there may have been too much attention paid to the president's wife by Rafinesque. The outcome was that Rafinesque was very upset after devoting ten years to Transylvania College. He swore that nothing of his should ever become a part of the college and today there is a locked room dedicated to his works but everything in there is copied and nothing original.

He went to Philadelphia by river and lived there until his death. He was placed in a pauper's grave. Only copies of his sticks are on file there and no one seems to know what happened to the Walam Olam sticks. Transylvania, at a later date to add insult to his name, dug up the pauper's grave and placed his bones under the college's steps to the Rathskeller and certain students are permitted to sleep on the steps on a celebration day each year. Rafinesque got the last laugh as the grave diggers dug the wrong pauper and Rafinesque's bones and the Walam Olam sticks remain in Philadelphia.

Today everyone who is reading this book has sung at least one of these songs from one of these sticks. Old King Cole is one of these early kings and the story of what he did during his life. The king was King Coel who was lost along with both King Arthurs in history when the

English discredited the ancient British history. Allowing the ancient king line to exist along with the Coelbren alphabet would bring attention to the fact that the English had stolen the king line in the fourteenth century from the British / Welsh. King Arthur could be romanticized as only a myth or legend and thus the world thinks there never was a real King Arthur let alone the fact that he came to this continent with his alphabet.

Chapter Three

1. Lilly, *The Walam Olam*, 1840.
2. *Bardus*, Recopied in 1640.

Chapter Four

The "All-Seeing Eye of God"

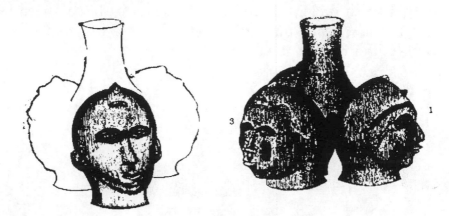

Triune Vessel with All-Seeing Eye of God

This triune vessel was found in a cave on the Cumberland River where two mummies were also found. It was in the home of John Clifford, a friend of Rafinesque, in 1820. It is a three-headed jug with predominant eyes. There were other three-headed jugs found on this continent but this one is especially important because of the eye motif. We showed this picture to Dr. Mary Powell, University of Kentucky archaeologist, and asked her what she made of it. She said that it "was definitely not Native American." There were other three-headed objects as seen on the next page, but none had the predominant eyes or the "all-seeing-eyes of God." The ancients felt that God sees the tiny sparrow fall in the forest as in the bible.

Cooper Stone

Three-Headed Jug with Awen

On this page are two examples of three-headed objects from this continent. The Cooper stone has three heads but you must hold it in your hands and turn it up or down to see all three. The Awen tells us who created the heads and the jug. The lady on page # 31 has recreated an ancient Indian jug with three faces and you can see the Awen in the center of the jug.

Other examples of the "All-Seeing Eye of God" are shown below. This first motif is often called the weeping eye.

Circle-Cross with Weeping Eye

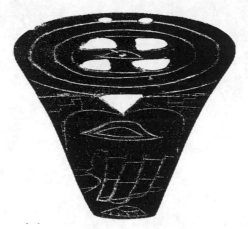

Circle-Cross with Eye

On page #32, the two-eye images are involved with the circle-cross which is a symbol with its own ancient meaning.

Eye in Open Hand

These are examples found across our continent from the Etowah mounds of Georgia to Moundville, Alabama. But how can we say that they are the "All-Seeing Eye of God?" This work was done for us by Joseph Campbell. He tracked the small statues seen on the next page. They start at Ur in the Mesopotamian area and proceed through the Mediterranean to the British Isles. [#1]

We are told by the Old Testament that Abraham left Ur and, as you can see from Campbell's work, he brought several things with him. He brought the "All-Seeing Eye of God" as well as the chevrons. We feel quite comfortable that he also brought the Coelbren alphabet and the swastika which will be explained in later chapters. We are not sure that Campbell knew the real significance of his finding but he was very positive in his presentation of this material and, as the reader can see, it all fits.

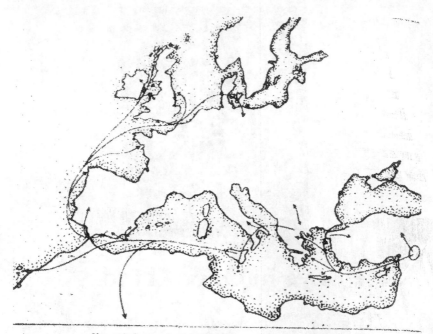

Map 7 Diffusion of Eye-Goddess, Monuments and Tradition from S.W. Asian Matrix via sea routes to N.W. African and W. European zones.

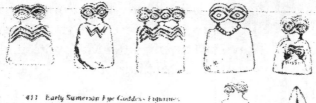

411 Early Sumerian Eye-Goddess Figurines, 3500-3000 B.C. Northwest Syria

Votive figurines of black or white alabaster, from strata deep beneath a temple floor of ca. 2800 B.C. See also Fig. 248

Joseph Campbell's Map

This is where Joseph Campbell's research ends and the Ancient Kentucke Historical Association's research begins. In 1992, Jim Michael went to Wales in search of several things. He wanted to see if there was a tie-in to the three-headed figure with four eyes in the wall joist of the Llandiff Cathedral in Cardiff, the capital of Wales. Everywhere he went in the cathedral, the eyes followed. The artist that had created this motif was very skillful. These three-headed structures were the "All-Seeing Eyes of God." These three-headed items were ordered destroyed by the Roman church as they were thought to be pagan or Gnostic. [#2]

Three heads with Four Eyes

The three-headed motif was found in many places where the ancient Brits had been. They were on jugs, stones and in a well in Kent. An archaeologist named Brian Slade found as many as 100 three-headed items in the well shown on the next page. Not knowing what he had, he chose to name it the Well of the Triple Goddess based on one of the triple heads shone here. [#3]

From the Well of the Triple Goddess

While Brian Slade has labeled this as Roman, as the English seem to want, it is ancient British in our and Wilson and Blackett's opinion. The serpent is Yahweh, the sword is power or military might. The banner is nationality or country and the torch is equality. The Gnostic and ancient Brits did everything in threes as all of this indicates. This is ancient British and not Roman.

Over one hundred three-headed items were found in this well and we feel that they are pre-Roman but thought to be anything but ancient British. It is almost as if the ancient British never existed. We wonder why?

Opening of the Well

The three heads, the "All-Seeing Eye," the chevrons, the circle-crosses are all ancient Amerindian symbols which are further proof of the archeological philosophy of diffusion rather than independent invention. It is also important to recognize the presence of the good serpent Yahweh on page #33 as well as on page #36. This is a two-continent diffusional tie-in.

Chapter Four

#1. Campbell, *The Mythic Image*, Princeton, N.J.1974.
#2. Michael, *Ancient Kentucke Inscriptions*, Chicago Spectrum Press, 2004.
#3. Slade, *The Well of the Triple Goddess Minister Abbey*, Santa Maria Publications, Kent, England, 1993.

Chapter Five

The Chevron among the Amerindian Symbols

The three-stroke chevrons appear in many of the artworks created by the ancients. In Kentucky, they appear by themselves as well as inside the circle-cross.

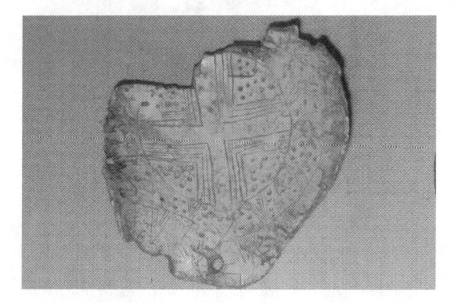

Shell found by William Webb

This is one of the items found by the head of the Archaeology Department of the University of Kentucky in 1935. Webb noted that there were chevrons as well as the circle-cross. This item is in the museum that caries his name at the University of Kentucky in Lexington, Kentucky. This item was found in the same area where many banner stones with chevrons were found. The banner stones were found by the sheriff of Augusta, Kentucky. He helped those who were digging in their yards for septic laterals and today has a huge collection of artifacts.

Replica of Cup found at Cahokia

The same chevron configuration was found in the center of a mound in Cahokia, Illinois. Only about five percent of the many Cahokia Mounds have been archaeologically examined, thus there is no way of knowing how many more artifacts still exist. As you will see on the next page, there is a very strong reason to believe that the circle-cross with the chevrons was an important religious symbol to the ancient British.

As the reader saw in chapter two, the chevron was brought out of the Mesopotamian area along with the All-Seeing Eyes of God by Abraham and his people. The chevron has an even older origin as the Bible talks of the tribes carrying their chevrons into battle. They are still used today in Cardiff, Wales as the coat of arms of the city of Cardiff, just as they were in King Arthur's day.

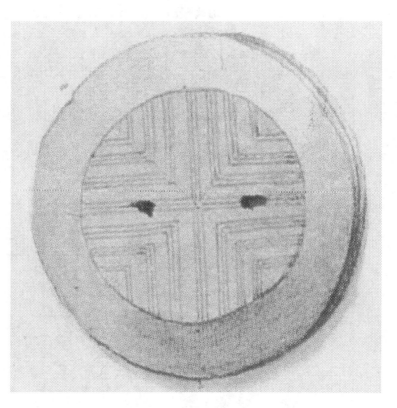

Gold Button Found at Stonehenge

It becomes obvious that the chevrons that we see inside the circle-cross have been diffused from the old world to the new and not independently invented. In the next chapter the reader will find that the circle-cross also has an important origin and meaning. Just because the same symbol was found at Cahokia Mounds, we do not mean to imply that all of the inhabitants of Cahokia were British or that they were the actual builders of the mound complex. The Brits did bury their dead in mounds and the concept could have its origin with their ancestors. The cross with chevrons goes back to Troy and was brought to the Tin Islands with the Trojans and Khumry and then on to this continent. [See page 52]

Window of Llandiff Cathedral Cardiff Wales

The coat of arms of King Meurig, the founder of the Llandiff Cathedral, can be seen above his head in the stained-glass window. King Meurig is an Uthur Pen Dragon and father of King Arthur II. Meurig is holding the church's charter. On the actual charter is King Meurig and below his name is the name Madoc.

The chevron coat of arms was, therefore, the coat of arms of King Arthur as well as the coat of arms of his brother Prince Madoc. Since we know that both of these men were on this continent, we see how the chevron arrived.

On the next page, you will see another example of the chevrons on a flag from the 1400s. The flag is the flag of Cardiff Castle. Note that the Welsh dragon also appears on the flag along with the chevrons. Today the chevrons are the coat of arms of Cardiff, the capital of Wales. The cross with chevrons is still used by the Vatican, but we are not sure they know why. [See picture on page 44.]

The Flag of Cardiff Castle

A striking tribute to wear close to your heart...

THE POPE
JOHN PAUL II
CROSS

Enlarged to show detail.
Actual size of cross is
1⅛" in height.

Cross with Chevrons Still Used Today

Chapter Five

1. Webb, *Ancient Life in Kentucky*, 1928.

Chapter Six

The Circle-Cross

In the last chapters, you have seen many examples of circle-crosses with the all-seeing eye of God as well as the chevrons. This motif is all over the American continent. Today, many of the Amerindian paintings and dress have this motif. We have seen it also in many of the British graveyards with the ancient tombstones.

The circle-cross can be found all through the Mediterranean. The flag of Greece is a circle-cross and it can also be found in the Egyptian hieroglyphs.

In 1991, Jim Michael went to Britain to check out the circle-cross. He found that, before the sixth century, the tombstones all had a circle-cross but after the seventh century, the cross began to come out of the circle. It seemed to have a Christian connotation after that time and something else prior. The ancient Brits were Christian. In fact, they were the first country to become Christian and are seated first by the Vatican today.

It was quite obvious that the circle-cross had an older pedigree than the Christian connotation. It wasn't until 1992 that he asked Alan Wilson to explain its origin. He drew the sketch that you will see on page #47 while he was in Louisville, Kentucky for a lecture tour.

He explained that the circle-cross was the zodiac as seen in the sky in the Mesopotamian area. The circle is made up of the twelve constellations in the night sky with Polaris in the center. When you draw an imaginary line from Orion to Taurus and from the Eagle to Leo, they intersect in the center at Polaris. This makes the circle-cross. This does not work in the northern hemisphere of the American continent yet the North American Indians all have and use the circle-cross.

William Webb's Circle-Cross

This is the actual composite stone that William Webb found at Fox Field near Augusta, Kentucky and is in the William Webb museum in Lexington, Kentucky. The top holes make this appear to be a gorget and make the cross appear to be not straight up and down. In Britain not all ancient circle-crosses are straight up and down. This was shown in *Ancient Kentucke Inscriptions*, pp. 108–109. [#1]

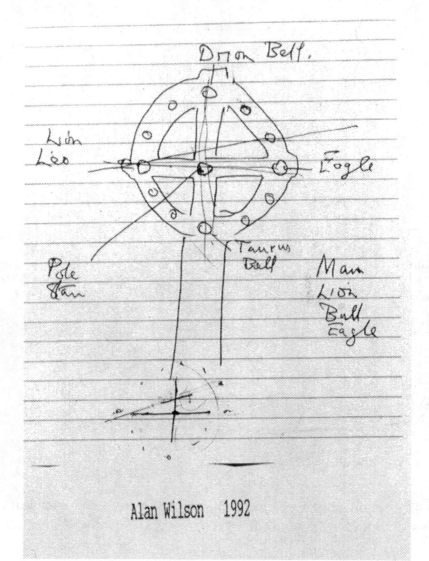

Alan Wilson 1992

Alan Wilson's Sketch

Alan also said that if we were to draw lines diagonally through Polaris, we would have the English flag.

Jim Michael was giving four presentations for the Generations of Faith series at St. Patrick Church in Louisville, Kentucky and after the second presentation, he remembered seeing those same animal names in the bible. And sure enough, when he turned to Ezekiel 1–10, there they were. Some bibles have dropped the animals because they don't understand their significance.

Ezekiel's vision of four wheels bearing the faces of a man, a lion, an ox, and an eagle.

The above author had all the correct animals but said that Ezekiel must have been having a schizophrenic hallucination. [#2] Ezekiel was one of the brightest men of his time and he was not having a schizophrenic problem that night in the eighth century B.C. in the Mesopotamian desert. **The circle that he saw "way up in the middle of the sky" was the circle-cross**. This is one symbol that Abraham did not bring out from the Mesopotamian area.

48

The circle-cross religious symbol can be found among many of the Amerindian tribes from coast to coast today. It is as important to these tribal members as it was to the ancients Brits who brought it to them in the sixth century.

Chapter Six

#1. Michael, *Ancient Kentucke Inscriptions, Prince Madoc Fact or Fiction*, Chicago Spectrum Press, 2004.
#2. *Mysteries of the Bible*, Time Life.

Chapter Seven

The Swastika of the Amerindians

When Jim Michael was a boy in Sioux City, Iowa, he had an Indian blanket on his bed which he loved. This was during the Second World War and the blanket had a swastika on it that was a mirror image of the Nazi swastika that had been adopted by Hitler as the Nazi's insignia. The question that he asked his parents was how could the Native Americans have used such a terrible symbol?

If you look up the word swastika in the Britannica Encyclopedia, it will tell you that it is an ancient symbol with some obscure religious significance. No one in Europe seams to know what the origin of the swastika really is.

Chief Samuel Brown

There seemed to be no good answer to this dilemma. The answer came from Yuchi Chief Sam Brown.

Chief Brown told Dr. Joseph B. Mahan in the 1950s that the "swastika denoted the Breath Master." Dr. Mahan, an anthropologist, recorded this in his book *The Secret* in 1983. The question is who is the Breath Master? (Chief Brown's picture is on the cover of *The Secret*.) [#1]

Saint Thomas, in the Bible, said "after we made man, the Holy Ghost breathed life into him." We believe that the Breath Master is the Holy Ghost. Thus, the swastika is the Holy Ghost. The swastika can be found along with the circle-cross in Europe in ancient times. Below they appear together.

An Irish Tombstone

We don't know the date of this stone but it was far earlier than the Second World War and the swastika is the mirror image of the Native American symbol. The question again is why is it reversed just like the German swastika? This becomes the next mystery for us to solve. While the swastika on the tombstone is older than World War II, it still has an older pedigree.

Grave Amulet from Troy

Here you see a mirrored swastika from the same province from which Brith came after the fall of Troy. Brith led the migration from the Mediterranean to the Tin Islands in 600 B.C. and became the first king of the long line of British kings. He also gave his name to the Britons.

The reader will now also see the combination of the cross and the chevrons along with the mirrored image of the swastika from perhaps 600 B.C. In the fourth chapter, we learned that the all-seeing eye of God and the chevrons came from Ur and Abraham came from Ur. We can then assume that these same people brought the swastika from Ur. By solving the mystery of the reversed swastika, we might be able to prove that the swastika came with the chevrons as well as the other symbols with Abraham and his followers. These followers of Abraham had been promised to be the chosen people on the earth and had a cohesiveness that bonded them together. They were called the Khumry which means kinsmen in their language. When Alan Wilson, British historian, was asked if they were Hebrew, he replied that Hebrew means wanderer in Khumric and that is exactly what they proved to be.

Picture by Dr. Lee Pennington

Canyon DeChelly

Back in the USA, in the Western cliff dweller area, we see again a mirror image of the swastika. A close-up of this will be seen on the next page. Our Native American advisor, Loren Jeffries, advised us that this was the symbol of the Anasazi. Jeffries was married to a Navaho woman and lived among the pueblo peoples.

Another great American mystery is why the Anasazi people left their homes with food still on their tables. The archaeologists have several speculative theories but no definitive answers. They found a lack of doors but openings in the ceilings with ladders that might imply that they were protecting themselves from something or someone, but who? They found human protein in the stool deposits that might mean cannibalism. But this does not fit with any of the traditions of this area. They found evidence of droughts but the ancients withstood droughts before.

Picture by Dr. Lee Pennington

Close-up of Swastika

54

Fertile Crescent

Abraham left Ur [at the bottom in the desert], followed the Euphrates, and took the chevrons, the all-seeing eye, and the Coelbren alphabet thru the Fertile Crescent to the rest of the world. The Sanskrit language and alphabet went south to the Indus Valley and on to India. The swastika went with the Sanskrit, proving the swastika left Ur with Abraham with the other symbols.

In Sanskrit the swastika means:

- Well Being
- Positive Being
- Found on Buddha and in his footsteps

Thus it provides us with the original meaning of the swastika which may have been lost elsewhere. [#2]

The most important finding is that the mirror image of the swastika in Sanskrit has a different meaning which is opposite to the positive implications of the original swastika. The mirror image has the following negative connotations:

- Darkness
- Misfortune
- Suffering
- Called Savustika

The rest of the world may have lost the real meaning of the mirror image of the swastika. On the tombstone and grave amulet, it is associated with death, darkness and misfortune. If this is the case, Hitler would have been well advised to use the original swastika, as the mirror image seems to have predicted his future outcome.

The Yuchi obviously knew the original meaning of the swastika and used it in a positive manor. The Anasazi may also have known the meaning of the mirror image of the swastika and were telling their people and the world that they were experiencing suffering, misfortune and darkness. If this is the case, the Ancient Kentucke Historical Association has found the reason why they abandoned their homes with food still on the table.

Chapter Seven

#1. Mahan, *The Secret*, Star Printing Co. Georgia, 1983.

#2. Liungman, *Dictionary of Symbols*, ABC–CLIO, 1991.

Chapter Eight

Which Way Did They Go?

In the last chapter, we started with the hypothesis that the symbols came out of Mesopotamia with Abraham with the swastika going to India. What if all the symbols came from India and spread throughout the world? A very good case can be made for this new hypothesis.

In 1990, Jim Michael presented an AKHA program comparing the findings in India and the Indus Valley with findings in Mexico and South America. These are:

1. Corn
2. Plumbing
3. Toys
4. Games

We have always considered corn as an American product, yet it can be seen in the hands of Shiva in the Indian temples. How could the ears of corn have been transported back to India from America? Could corn have come from India rather than developed by the American Indians as we have been taught?

The plumbing in the Indus Valley was piped by basalt gutters with flat basalt capstones just as in South America. Where did this concept develop?

Ancient Shiva [note corn in hand]

Corn in Shiva's Hand

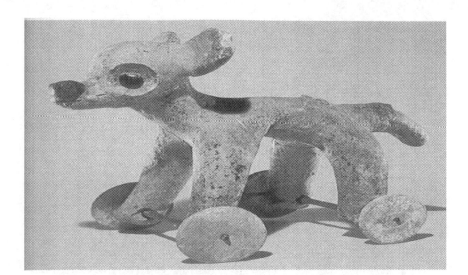

Toy from Veracruz [A.D.800-1200] # 1.

Toys from the Indus Valley # 2.

We were told that there were no wheels used for transportation on this continent. On this page, there are examples of wheels on toys. This concept is identical and not independently invented. The question remains which way did this concept diffuse? With the toys, it seems quite logical that they diffused from India to South America.

This brings us to the Royal game of India. The game has been played by most young children and is called Parcheesi. The Aztec's have the same board game but it is called Patolli. The question again is which way did it go?

In early 2006, Joseph Adams, research director for Ancient Kentucke Historical Association, presented some interesting information which indicated that the Garden of Eden or Edin may have been in the Indus Valley rather than the traditional location of Iraq. He presented the map of Alexander the Great's withdrawal through the Indus Valley. The map from L.A. Waddell's book was the most intriguing part of his presentation.

A copy of this map is on page #56 and if you look at the ancient city of Mohenjo Daro, you can see the large area of EDIN going through the valley. Is it possible that this is the starting point of the EDEN of Genesis and not the long accepted site of the Mesopotamian valley?

If this is the case, Waddell may well have unknowingly given us the truth of the Indus enigma. This, however, opens even more questions as to how this was covered up and we think that it was covered up? Just as the Irish, Scots and Welsh had their ancient history distorted and hidden away for over a thousand years by the English victors, the same could have been reshaped for India's history by the English.

In November of 2006, Dr. Warner Sizemore presented his AKHA program *When India Ruled the World.* He explained that India did, in fact, have a navy and could very well have sailed the world. There are those who feel that Sanskrit is the oldest language and is a language through which all other languages can be translated.

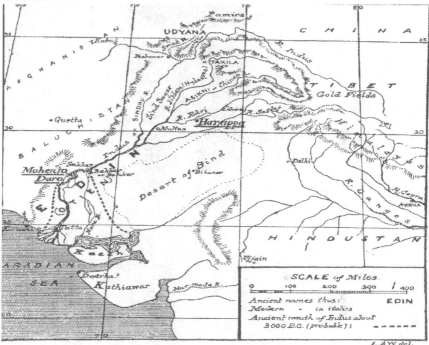

Map of Indus Valley, showing " Find " sites of Seals.

[Note] EDIN

In his handout, Dr. Sizemore revealed the most interesting clue of all. It ties this all together. It is the Tibetan Naga number system compared with the Mayan.
#3

	Naga	**Maya**
#1.	Hun	Hun
#2.	Cas	Ca
#3.	Ox	Ox
#4.	San	Can
#5.	Ho	Ho
#6.	Usac	Uax
#7.	Usc	Usc
#8.	Uax	Uaxac
#9.	Bolan	Bolon
#10.	Lahun	Lahun

Now there is no question as to who the Mayan people are and the diffusion of this number system but again the question is which way did it diffuse?

Chapter Eight

#1. Readers Digest, *Mysteries of the Ancient Americas*, 1986.
#2. Thompson, *Nu Sun*, 1989.
#3. Matlock, *Once India Ruled the Americas*, 2000.

Chapter Nine
Navaho Sand Painting

The Navaho shaman is summoned to the home of a tribal member who is sick and in need of healing. The shaman spreads sand on the floor of the home and begins to create a design on it with colored sand. He or she calls on the healing power of the entire world in this painting. This is a typical Navaho sand painting.

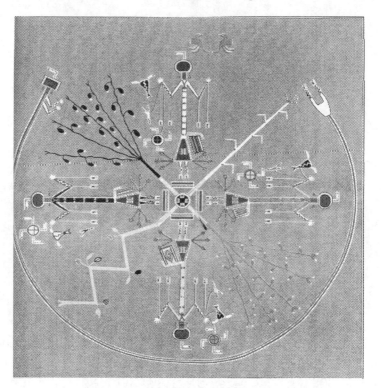

Navaho Sand Painting

The Circle is the Earth-Mother-Father and the shaman calls on the healing of the whole world. The shaman places the ill individual on the painting and begins his chanting which may last for the most of a week. To understand what he has drawn, we will examine the top fourth of the painting.

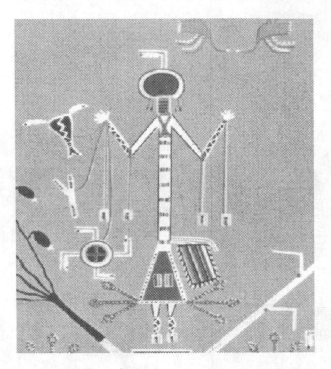

Top 1/4th of the painting

As we look at the top shaman in this portion of the sand painting, we can start to see many of the symbols that we have been studying in this book. The first symbol is Ezekiel's wheel [the circle-cross] which is surrounded by the positive Swastika or the Breath Master — the Holy Ghost. Next, you will note at the edge of the shaman's skirt the three-stroke Awen sign for God or Yahweh. The shaman has called on the highest power that is known to the Navaho people. The power of this situation must be very spiritual.

There is one more symbol which is held by a string to the left of the shaman. It is a two-headed snake. The question here is what could this symbol be and what does it have to do with healing? The obvious answer, which is speculation, is that it might be the caduceus. The military incorrectly uses the staff of Hermes on their medical uniforms.

Hermes was the Greek God of the underworld. He was responsible for transporting the soul to its final resting place. Here is an example of the use of this staff.

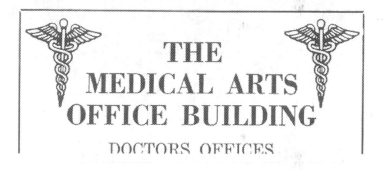

THE MEDICAL ARTS OFFICE BUILDING
DOCTORS OFFICES

The Staff of Hermes

The Ancient Kentucke Historical Association feels that the staff of Hermes is being used incorrectly. Perhaps they don't understand that it is not correct. The fact is, because it has been used this way for so long, people believe it to be correctly used without understanding its origin.

We feel that the correct staff of the medical community should be the staff of Asclepius. The Greek God Asclepius was the greatest healer of all time. This,

65

therefore, could be the healer symbol that has been used by the Navaho shamans. He/she could be calling on the power of the greatest healer of all times.

Staff of Asclepius

The Ancient Kentucke Historical Association feels that this is the right use of the staff of Asclepius and that the Navaho shaman used it to focus the greatest healing possible to his patients. We wondered how a Greek could get into the Gnostic symbols until we found the Gospel of Asclepius in the Gnostic Bible. [#1]

Asclepius must have held an important position among the Khumry in order to have his writings preserved for us by them. Today we have his spiritual body functions recorded along with his religious position on they way to reach heaven through good deeds. Although St Paul also said the Gnostics were persecuted for this. Thus the caduceus among the Navaho is quite in keeping with the other symbols.

The symbols used by the Amerindians display the European diffusion. We have presented overwhelming evidence of this and defeated all of the skeptics who have continued to believe that the Amerindian symbols were the product of independent invention.

Chapter Nine

#1. Robertson, *The Nag Hammadi Library in English*, 1988.

Chapter Ten

DNA and its Implications

While the diffusion of the Amerindian symbols remains a speculative proof to the mainstream archaeologists, the DNA enters into the equation in the twenty-first century. The DNA is very hard for scholars to disprove and once it penetrates the membrane of impossibilities, the cultural lag of true facts becomes a possibility.

The Smithsonian's archaeologists took a good look at the Solutrean points and how they were made in France 18,000 years ago and started to see how the Solutreans could have traveled to this continent and created the Clovis point. This started the chain of events that crumbled the "Clovis First theory," the "ice corridor for the first Americans," the "no European contact prior to Columbus," and opened the door for the first time to the concept of "ancient ocean travel."

As the twenty-first century progresses with this open door, the content of this book will have to move the Amerindian symbols to the level of empiric value along with North American epigraphy. Adding greater impact to this shift in mind-set are the discovery by French archaeologists of 50,000-year-old tools and the Mexican archaeologist's 13,500-year-old skeletons that are not Native American and were in Mexico prior to the Ice Age corridor.

The individuals who peopled the South American continent turned out to be the same people who populated the Pacific Islands 50,000 to 60,000 years ago without benefit of a land bridge. If they could get to

Tahiti, Easter Island and Hawaii by boat, why couldn't they get to the South American continent in the same manner? Thus, we have the shift of a 100-year-old mind-set and the ending of this archaeological conservative culture lag.

The DNA evidence which Jim Michael presented in his book *Ancient Kentucke Inscriptions* was from West Virginia. [#1]

Dr. Robert L. Pyle

Dr. Pyle is a geologist and holds an archaeological certification which he received while working for the West Virginia Highway Department. He served as the state archaeologist for West Virginia. He became interested in a shelter inscription some years ago and found a skeleton in the shelter near one of the epigraphs. The laboratory carbon 14 date showed it to be A.D. 710 +/- 40 years. The DNA has a haplogene X that comes from Europe. Although Pyle taught at the Smithsonian Institution [Department of Energy] and had approval to announce his findings in AD 2000, they dragged their feet. There was pressure not to publish; therefore, they never published these important findings.

Dr. Pyle gave up on the Smithsonian and sent the information to Ancient American magazine for publication. It appeared on the cover of Volume #9 in 2004. This was a breakthrough in getting this type of information out to the American people. The Kennewick Man and the Spirit Cave Man, long thought to be non-Native American, have been brushed aside and covered up by our government. [#2]

This has spurred a large study of this Haplogene in Native Americans. To date, this study has amassed over 70,000 cultures from the Native American tribes. The findings are overwhelming and the study is ongoing. For a better understanding of the study, the article written by Jim Michael is included on the following pages.

The study is a mitochondrial DNA or mtDNA composite completed by swabbing the mouths of Native Americans from many tribes. Although there are tribes that have been omitted, it is only because they have not completed adequate sampling to add the tribe to the list. For example, the Navaho tribe has been added to the list. The Haplogene Groups A, B, C and D can trace their haplogroup back across the Bering Straits to the Siberian continent. The haplogroup X came from Europe and thus the Ancient Kentucke Historical Association can prove that there was European contact before Columbus.

North American Native Americans and Mitochondrial DNA

Jim Michael, Ancient Kentucke Historian

The early studies of North American Indians by Brigham Young University using mitochondrial DNA or mtDNA has shown four major clades or haplogroups. These four haplogroups A, B, C and D exhibit significant regional patterning among native populations of North America and are broadly distributed throughout the Americas. All four of these haplogroups are shared with Asian populations thus providing proof of the conclusion long postulated that early migration took place across the Bering land bridge.

Not all the mtDNA falls into these four haplogroups. In several studies, similar sequences appear to fall into a fifth group. Investigators are calling the fifth group haplogroup X. This group apparently shares a matrilineal ancestor with the European ancestor at some time in prehistory (before Columbus).

The haplogroup X can be found among the Mandan, Osage, Dakota, Chippewe/Ojibway, Pomo, Yakima, Cheyenne/Arapaho, Blackfeet, Shawnee, Mimac, Jemez, Kiowa, Nootka, Tuscaroras, Abnake, Anishinabeg,

Delaware/Lenape, Etchemis, Malisett, Micmac, Mohegan, Narraganset, Passamaquoddy, Penobscott, Quinnipiac and Wabanski. The most intriguing fact is that the Algonquian tribal lineage has nearly 20% haplogroup X. It becomes quite obvious by following haplogroup X that there was a great deal of splitting off of new tribal groups and wife exchanging with other tribes.

BYU now has developed a pool of worldwide DNA patterns. This is how in 2001 they could tell that the seventh-century remains of the West Virginia individual's mtDNA could be traced to the British Isles as reported in *The Ancient American.*

These studies will end speculation and supposition of archaeological human bone findings. It will be very hard for the mainstream academics to say that there was no European contact with the Americas prior to Columbus.

References:

1. Michael, *Ancient Kentucke Newsletter,* Oct. 2004.
2. Duke & Morgan, The Multiple Origins of the North American Indians, April 2004
3. Eshleman, Mitochondrial DNA of the North American Indians, *Evol Anthropol*, 12:7-18, 2003.
4. Malhi, Haplogroup X confirmed in North America, *Am. Jl. Phys. Anthropol*, 119:84-86, 2002.
5. Smith, Distribution of mtDNA Haplogroup X Among Native North Americans, *Am. Jl. Psy. Anthropol*, 110:271-284, 1999.
6. Pyle, *Ancient American*, Vol.9, Nr. 56. 2004.
7. Michael, *Ancient Kentucke Inscriptions*, Dec. 2004.

8. Michael, *Ancient Kentucke Newsletter*, Oct. 2004.
9. Duke & Morgan, *The Multiple Origins of the North American Indians*, April 2004
10. Eshleman, *Mitochondrial DNA of the North American Indians*, *Evol Anthropol*, 12:7-18, 2003.
11. Malhi, *Haplogroup X confirmed in North America*, *Am. Jl. Phys. Anthropol*, 119:84-86, 2002.
12. Smith, *Distribution of mtDNA Haplogroup X Among Native North Americans*, *Am. Jl. Psy. Anthropol*, 110:271-284, 1999.
13. Pyle, *Ancient American*, Vol.9, Nr. 56. 2004.
14. Michael, *Ancient Kentucke Inscriptions*, Dec. 2004.

■ Republished in the fall of 2004 in *Journal of the Falls of the Ohio Archaeological Society*, Volume 2 number 2, *p #95*. [#3]

The finding of the DNA haplogroup X started quite a dilemma for the members of the Mormon Church. Joseph Smith, the church's patriarch and prophet, had said that the Native Americans were the principal ancestors of the lost tribes of Israel. When evidence showed that most of the ancestors of the Native Americans came across the Bering Straits and only a small portion came from Europe, they thought Smith not to be the prophet they had acknowledged him to be.

When Christopher Columbus returned to Europe with Native Americans on board, the Pope announced that they were the descendants of the Ten Lost Tribes of Israel. This was the way for the Pope to account for humans who were new to the knowledge of the world.

In the 1830s, Joseph Smith simply repeated this premise. There was a big split in the Mormon Church because of this DNA finding and it is possible that his followers did not know that Smith had, perhaps, quoted the Pope.

It is interesting to point out that the haplogroup X is the link to the ancient Israelites. The ancient Brits were descendants of the "House of David" and "Sons of Israel." While the minority of DNA was X, the Native Americans carried the DNA which will go back to Solomon and then back to Abraham. Joseph Smith was absolutely correct when he said that Native Americans were the descendants of the Israelites. The problem is with the words "sole" or "principal" when applied to the word "ancestors."

Chapter Ten

#1. Michael, *Ancient Kentucke Inscriptions*. Chicago Spectrum Press. 2004.
#2. Pyle, *Ancient American*, Vol.9, Nr. 56. 2004.
#3. Michael, *Journal of the Falls of the Ohio Archaeological Society*, Volume 2 number 2, p #95.

Chapter Eleven

Close but no Cigar

It is easy to be a Monday morning quarterback when you know the outcome. Now when we know that the Brits were here in the sixth century, we can look back at the people who speculated about it and see how close they were. There were two authors that need recognition.

The first author who almost had the answer was Josiah Priest in 1835. He did little personal investigation but wrote and recorded many enigmas from all over the United States. He was a contemporary of Rafinesque but had no contact that we can determine. One of the subjects was about a mummy that was found in Florida that had an alphabetic inscription. He reported that the mummy was visited by a Scottish author who recognized the alphabet as that which was written on metal in a cemetery in the Hebrides Islands off the coast of Scotland. [#1]

If anyone had followed up on this correctly, it would have made all our work unnecessary. They would have found the alphabet to be Coelbren and would have identified the mummies as being created by the ancient Brits.

The follow-up was attempted by Dr. Samuel Mitchell who wrote to Scotland and asked for help to identify the mummies that were found in Kentucky. He went into great detail to describe the mummies but failed to ask about the alphabet and where it was found. We are assuming that the reason that he wrote to Scotland was because of Priest's article in his book. The answer was obviously negative as the Scotts had not been involved in mummification for thousands of years. The Scottish people's lineage goes back to the Scythians and the Scythians did practice mummification in the Urals in ancient times.

The Coelbren alphabet was the alphabet of the Bards and Druids of France and Britain. The alphabet is on stones all over the British Islands. It can be found in the Bodleian Library in Oxford. It was on coins even before the birth of Jesus Christ and should have been recognized as this would have solved the biggest dilemma of American history. The Coelbren alphabet has been recognized and translated in over 60 inscriptions on the North American continent. Examples can be seen in *Ancient Kentucke Inscriptions* [#2] and the others can all be seen in the *King Arthur Conspiracy* [#3]. An additional important inscription can be seen in Chapter twelve of this book.

The next author was the first president of the Filson Club, Reuben Durrett. [The Filson Club is the historical society of Louisville, Ky.] In his appendix, he noted that the Archbishop of Canterbury had stated that King Arthur had knowledge of this continent and that a Welsh prince had told him about it. Durrett had the key in his hands but without the research available to him that we have today, he did not have the resources to pull this all together. [#4]

The Archbishop of Canterbury, George Abbott, did write this in 1625 and he and Durrett had the key in their hands but let it slip right through. John Williams who Durrett mentions in his book also makes the same statement that King Arthur knew of this continent and that a prince had told him about it. He also states that the prince was Prince Madoc.

So you see, both Priest and Durrett had the brass ring but neither could pull it loose. They were both close but no cigar.

Chapter Eleven

#1. Priest, *American Antiquities and Discoveries in the West*, 1833.

#2. Michael, *Ancient Kentucke Inscriptions*, Chicago Spectrum Press, Dec. 2004.

#3. Berkley, *The King Arthur Conspiracy*, Trafford Press, Canada, 2005.

#4. Durrett, *Traditions of the Earliest Visits of Foreigners to North America*, London, 1906.

Chapter Twelve

Spirituality of the Ancients

The Ancient Kentucke Historical Association does not have a religious agenda in researching the ancients. However, once we established that the ancients who came to this continent were devoutly religious, it was imperative to understand their thinking in order to enlighten our followers and all who read our findings. Along the way, it was also imperative to understand their motivational feelings as well as their religion.

Once that we understood that they were Gnostic Christian, it behooved us to separate them from the rest of the Christians or Orthodox Christians, as Constantine chose to call them. When Constantine called the Nicene Counsel in A.D. 325, the three Druids from Britannia were seated first. Britannia was the first to become a Christian country and is today still seated first in all Roman Catholic assemblies.

The Druids followed their Old Testament to the letter as we have explained in this book. When it came time to vote on the unification of the Church, they went along with the agenda to a point. They voted positively on the council's proposals until they came to a stumbling block. The vote was on Jesus being God and it passed by a small margin. At that point, the three Druids rose and stated that they could not continue — ethically, morally and religiously. Jesus was either God or not God and that mortal man had no right to vote him one way or the other. The Druids withdrew and went back to Britannia.

If Constantine was officiating, he should have thrown the question out and the split would have been over. However, Constantine may not have been there to make this decision, and the Druids were allowed to depart. Constantine's mother, Helena, was a Gnostic Christian and thus there was no repercussion against Britannia as there would be in future years against the Gnostics in the rest of the world.

The Christians in the rest of the world were given the option to join the Orthodox movement or be put to death. This does not sound like a Christian idea. Constantine was not yet a Christian. It wasn't until on his deathbed that he was baptized. Some feel that he did this only to become a saint in the Roman Church. The Greek Orthodox Church, not the Roman Catholic Church, made Constantine a saint.

It was quite disturbing to a member of the AKHA to read of the early atrocities and to read the books left out of today's Bible. Partially for these reasons she actually left the Roman Church. Yes, the early Church had a struggle over which scripts to include and the best way to officiate. That does not make it wrong but instead points to the fallibility of man. This should not be taken as a flaw in any religion.

The Gnostics were as spiritual as any Christians. They appear to have taken a different pathway toward allowing women to officiate in their religious practice. The Druids had female priests. The Native Americans had female shamans as a result of the diffusion of the Gnostics. Yet the Old Testament was written by the two Hebrew tribes which Nebuchadnezzar removed to Mesopotamia [Judea and Benjamin plus some of the Levites.] This, we think, is the origin of not allowing women to officiate in the church.

In order to get into the mind of the ancient Brits who were on this continent in the sixth century and perhaps before, we have to understand the Gnostic mind. One way to do this is to examine the Gnostic Bible or *Nag Hammadi Bible* as some have called it. Because they had a different biblical orientation, this did not make them any less spiritual. It is ignorant to deny that there were ancient writings in the first centuries after Christ. It would be equally arrogant of us to think of them as unimportant to those who wrote them and believed in them. [# 1]

We can understand the great pressure of the church to standardize the early writings into acceptable texts. The early Christians had many beliefs concerning what Christianity should be and wrote down what all of the early players thought and spoke. The Gnostics had many such writings which they called Gospels. These good news writings were the way they interpreted the Christian events. At the early councils of Carthage and Hippo, different bishops presented their lists of which books or gospels should be canonized.

I am sure that each argued the case for his own list. When the dust settled and the selections were confirmed, the non-selected books fell into obscurity. These should not be interpreted as bad or heretical books just because they were not accepted by the councils. There is a feeling that the selected books were somehow deified. Who is to say that the gospels of Thomas or Philip are more or less deified than that of Luke? Certainly the gospel of Jesus should be considered as deified. The gospel of Jesus was left off of the list perhaps because Jesus said that there was a great serpent in the sky. See next page for Serpens.

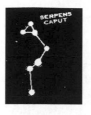

Serpens

The ancients were very involved with celestial events and there was a constellation called the Serpens. We are sure that some of the councilmen might not have wanted astrology to be a Christian event. The ancient Hebrews believed that the sun stood still for Joshua and that their menorah was based on a seven-night light experience in the heavens. But this might confuse Christianity and thus some, we are sure, might want this type of thing excluded. We feel that the Gnostics firmly believed in astrology.

We can't be certain who actually wrote the gospels attributed to the men that we call saints. How can we be sure that each accepted book is in fact divinely inspired? If we were to pick one that would be divinely inspired, we would have to choose the gospel of Jesus.

It becomes easy to call anyone who does not accept our beliefs as non-conformists. The early Hebrews called the non-believers heathens just as the Orthodox Christians called all other Christians heretics. This labeling does not imply any derogative connotation on the group labeled.

The members of the Ancient Kentucke Historical Association feel that the Gnostics may have been the true Hebrews "House of David" and the "Ten Tribes of Israel" that brought the Ark of the Covenant with them to Britain where it has been for 2,500 years. We feel that it will be found soon as a result of our British colleagues' research and if it is found in Britain, the Gnostics brought it there. If this is the case, the label of "heretic" given to the Gnostics by the early Church not only was wrong but was evidence of the church using political degradation to put down a religious group for political reasons. If the Ark is found, it presents a real dilemma to the Church who branded the "House of David" and "Ten Tribes of Israel" as heretics.

The belief of the Ancient Kentucke Historical Association that the Gnostic Christians were given an incorrect title of heretic is reflected in recently published literature. Now in the 21st century, many of the Gnostic books and gospels have been found and have made their way into mainstream literature. *The Da Vinci Code* is an example of a Gnostic gospel being expanded with fictional writing to make it believable and saleable. [# 2]

The Gospel of Thomas makes a case for Mary Magdalene being a teacher and disciple of Jesus, but does not imply a marriage partner. The visions that Saint Peter asked Mary to repeat to other followers of "the way" shows the chauvinistic feelings of the early saints but should not make Mary Magdalene a prostitute. The *Gospel of Judas* was an authentic early writing but does not imply correctness nor does it imply imperfections or heresy among Gnostic followers. To label these spiritual Christians as heretics is to do all readers a disservice. [# 3]

Thus we have a vast migration of these very spiritual individuals coming to the shores of this continent in the sixth century in seven hundred boats. They may have come earlier but we can prove sixth century empirically. One of the eight writings from the abbeys of Britain said that they sailed in the direction of the ancients. This statement causes Ancient Kentucke to regard the possibility of earlier migrations as very realistic and would explain the earlier carbon dates.

The spirituality and celestial orientation can be seen in many of the findings on the American continent. In the next chapter, we will examine the religious doctrine involved with the symbolism which came with their spirituality. We can also see the evidence of the celestial impact on their religion.

The ancient Hebrews saw the "Festival of Lights" as a celestial event that was the basis for the menorah of seven candles which is part of their religious doctrine. While this was also revered by the Romans as the "feast of light" named Saturnalia, Velikovsky suggests that this could be the explosion of Saturn that caused a seven-day light show on earth. [#4] The seven candles of the menorah were expanded by the eighth candle of Hanukkah which commemorates the "miracle of oil" during which an oil lamp with one day's amount of oil burned for eight days and nights.

On the next page can be seen an earthwork showing such a lamp and candles. This represents the days that the miraculous top lamp burned. The center candle is used in the ceremony to light the other candles.

This earthwork has been plowed away but, as you can see, it once touched the East fork of the Little Miami River in Ohio. This very large earthwork was surveyed by General Lytle of Cincinnati in 1825 and then his etching was included in Squire and Davis's *Ancient Monuments of the Mississippi Valley* in 1848. [# 5]

The Ancient Kentucke Historical Association has a very hard time explaining the Hanukkah earthwork as anything other than just what it shows. The large Awen symbol in the very large circle mound at Newark, Ohio

83

gives us an important tie-in to the builders of the Ohio earthwork. [See p. #5]

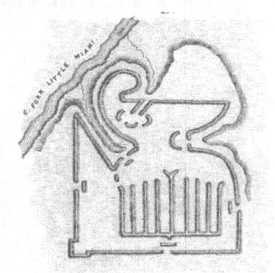

Hanukkah Earthwork in Ohio

The first question the casual observer who is reading all of this reconstructed historical research would ask is why didn't they just write and tell us who they were, when they came and why they expended so much effort to create such a large earthwork? The truth is that they did all of this and we, with our archaeological mind-set, choose to ignore all of the evidence. The mind-set of the American archaeologist is that there is no writing on the North American continent. We have translated over 60 messages carved in the bedrock of the country. One would think that one message would be adequate. [# 6]

The ancient Brits left sixth-century writings in the abbeys of Britain that tell us who they were, when they came and why they came. All of these were forgotten or incorrectly translated and kept from the British public to hide the fact that the English monarchy stole the kingship of the British-Welsh-Khumry in the 15th century.

If the Brits were here on this continent, then the one hundred and forty-year-old problem of the Decalogue stone should be an authentic artifact. There are just too many scholars, archaeologists, religious, and linguists who have denounced the Decalogue Stone as a forgery. We know that it seems impossible that the Ten Commandments could have been preserved here on the American continent. There is just too much contrary mind-set evidence that there was no contact in the Americas with Europe prior to Columbus and no alphabetic writing on the North American continent. Couple this with the wrong mind-set that no boats could make it to America before Columbus. But would it not be wonderful if the Decalogue Stone was the Ten Commandments and was authentic. It would further define the spirituality of the people who brought the religious symbols to the Amerindians.

Chapter Twelve

#1. Robertson, *The Nag Hammadi Library*, Harper & Row, 1988.
#2. Brown, *The Da Vinci Code*, Doubleday, 2003.
#3. Iscariot, *The Gospel of Judas*, National Geographic, 2006.
#4. Velikovsky, *Worlds in Collision*, Doubleday, 1950.
#5. Squier, *Ancient Monuments of the Mississippi Valley*, Smithsonian Institution Press, 1848, republished 1992.
#6. Berkley, *The King Arthur Conspiracy*, Trafford Press, 2005.

Chapter Thirteen

The Decalogue Stone: Fact or Forgery

For 145 years the pros and cons of this topic have been bantered back and forth. If this and the other holy stones were forged, they would not have been brought here with the symbols which we have already explored. If they are factual, they explain the presence of the religious symbols among the Amerindians.

The Decalogue Stone
One of the Holy Stones of Newark, Ohio

This story begins on June 29, 1860 when an amateur archaeologist and county land surveyor named David Wyrick found one of the holy stones in Newark, Ohio. He was looking in the woods near the large octagon. This octagon was part of the largest earthwork in the world. The earthwork had circles, a square and an octagon ranging from 20 to 40 acres each. There were paths or roadways connecting each. [#1]

Below is Squires and Davis's etching of this largest earthwork of its kind in the world. Most of this no longer exists but the bottom large circle and the square have been saved by the golf course owner who has a lease on the grounds for the next 70 years.

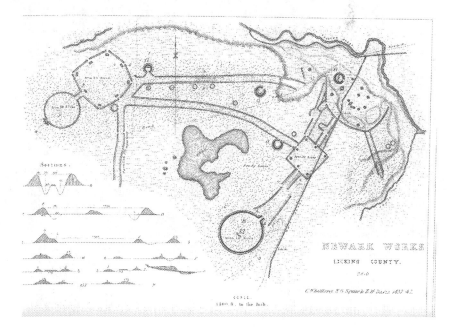

Newark Earthwork

As recorded by Squires and Davis [#2]

The Keystone
One of the Holy Stones of Newark, Ohio

The Keystone was the first stone that David Wyrick found in 1860 and, as you can see from the above picture, he thought it had Hebrew letters on all four sides. The letters certainly looked like Hebrew marks. He was quick to adopt a theory that the earthwork was the product of the Lost Ten Tribes of Israel. [#3]

This was the beginning of the controversy that has lasted for these last 145 years. In the same year, Rev. J. Austin Merrick, after examining the inscription on the Keystone, said that the Chaldee letters were the same as any forger could have found in the back of any Hebrew bible of this period.

David Wyrick and his small group of supporters had found, in a large mound nearby, the Decalogue Stone on November 1, 1860 and thought that this was the answer to the debate over the authenticity of the Keystone. Surely everyone would know now that this Hebrew tablet would convince the skeptics that the site was authentic. This stone was found in a forty foot mound under a wooden burial casket. To further complicate the matter, Rabbi Dr. Fischell read a paper before the American Ethnological Society on June 11, 1861 in which he presented the findings of the Decalogue Stone. He wrote that there were ten errors or imperfections in the inscriptions which caused him to conclude that the engraver of the stones "was neither a Hebrew nor a man of much knowledge."

David Wyrick, wanting to prove and confirm these findings, took a loan on his property of around $25 to travel to Cincinnati to confer with an expert. A confirmation would allow him to sell the stones to recoup the loan. The so-called expert declared the stones fake and eventually David lost his property. He took an overdose of Dilaudid, his arthritic medication. He died three years after finding the stones.

Today, archaeologist Dr. Bradley Leper tells the audience in a taped interview that things like this don't just happen this way. People don't just go out and find an additional piece of evidence that supports the original find. Therefore, the findings have to be discounted. In fact, in a letter dated September 15, 1991, Dr. Frank Cross, professor of Hebrew and other oriental languages at Harvard and one of the foremost scholars studying the Dead Sea Scrolls, stated the only possible explanation was that the Decalogue Stone was a "grotesque forgery."

One of the voices crying out in favor of the authenticity is Dr. J. Houston McCulloch, a professor of Economics and Finance at Ohio State University. While he is not in the field of linguistics, he has studied the Hebrew alphabet and states that some of the letters are as old as the Dead Sea Scrolls. Ancient Kentucke has also confirmed his findings and agrees that the letters are on the copper portion of the Dead Sea Scrolls. Both have been translated by Alan Wilson and Baram Blackett. The alphabet is Coelbren which became many other alphabets. [#4], [#5].

In 1992, Alan Wilson and Jim Michael were able to see some very poor pictures of the copper portion of the Dead Sea Scrolls at the Baptist Seminary in Louisville, Kentucky. The scroll letters were the same as the Decalogue Stone. It became obvious that the Decalogue Stone was not forged by David Wyrick or the dentist as had been speculated. It was then that the decision was made to re-examine the Holy Stones of Newark.

The Copper Portion of Dead Sea Scroll

One of the incorrect arguments used by archaeologist Dr. Bradley Leper is that the great die-off of the American Indians is a "one-time event and can only happen once." If this continent had been in contact with ancient Europeans, immunity would have developed against the diseases that had been brought here and would have prevented future Native Americans from dying off when the post-Columbians arrived after 1492. [#1] While this theory sounds good, it is not sound medical information. Acquired immunity is just that, and lasts only a generation or so. The body must be exposed again and again in order to acquire further immunity as we have painfully learned with the polio vaccine during this decade. Dr. Leper, in the same symposium, concluded that the "Holy Stones" of Newark "are fascinating windows into the rollicking formative years of the discipline of Archaeology" but the fact remains that "Archeologists, historians, and scholars of ancient Hebrew agree they are forgeries."

Dr. Hugh McCulloch realized that only about half of the letters on the Decalogue Stone are Hebrew. He admits that he doesn't understand why anyone would use such a strange alphabet and that he can't identify the alphabet. He is right in that it is the Ten Commandments in an abbreviated version and also that someone had to plan out the stone to get it all on. Where he missed was over the head of the man on the stone. He thought it said MUSE for Moses. We can see how he confused the F for an E. He would not know what MUSF meant. This word which is also abbreviated is not Hebrew but Khumric or Welsh.

Musf
Over the head of man on Decalogue Stone

MUSF translates into Khumric as "he of the basket," just as the unabbreviated MWSEFF on Moses' false door below. [Note the W or double U is a vowel in the Coelbren alphabet — in fact, the only vowel that is not also an English vowel.] MUSF is MOSES but no one on this continent could have known this. All the early and late investigators, including McCulloch, thought the alphabet was Hebrew. The fact that the order of the letters was reversed dates its creation as pre-Christian.

The false door of Mwseff or Moses, misidentified as Ptah-Shepses

The False Door of MWSEFF or MOSES

The translation of the false door of Moses or Mwseff, documents the use of "he of the basket" which describes Moses. Wilson and Blackett published this in 2006 in their book *Moses in the Hieroglyphics*. Their book exposes the fact that the so-called experts at the British Museum and Oxford can't really read the Egyptian hieroglyphics as they have claimed for so long. The Egyptian Egyptologists also must have egg on their faces as they have repeatedly said that English and American authors have no real understating of Egyptian history, while Alexander the Great, on display in the Cairo Museum, is misidentified because they can't read the hieroglyphics. [#6]

Once the reader understands the significance of the Twelve Tribes of Israel being the creators of the Egyptian hieroglyphics, it is easy to see how the key to translating the characters was lost. When Moses left Egypt in 1350 B.C. and later the Romans killed the Egyptian high priests, the knowledge of Khumric died out and so did the ability to read the so-called Egyptian hieroglyphics.

The translator must know the Khumric word for the glyph and then use the first syllable for that word to be able to translate it. While this sounds very simple, the Khumry or ten remaining Tribes of Israel kept such a low profile that this was almost forgotten. Several Welsh scholars have alluded to the fact that this could have been done throughout the centuries but no one except Blackett and Wilson took the time to translate the Egyptian hieroglyphics for the world.

The twenty years that it took the Ancient Kentucke Historical Association to prove that the Decalogue Stone is authentic could never have been done without the cooperation of our AKHA members Blackett and Wilson and their relentless step-by-step research of their forbidden history.

The Decalogue Stone is absolutely authentic, was created in a pre-Christian time, "should be in the older pre-Nebuchadnezzar era," [as per Blackett and Wilson] and had to be brought here from the Old World along with the ancient symbols surrounding their religion. It is not the product of any type of forgery by anyone living or dead.

Now the reader knows how the important symbols made it to the American continent and into the Native American religion and culture. This research supports the "diffusion" of concepts and defeats the "independent invention theory" at least of the religious symbolism as reported in this book.

Chapter Thirteen

#1. *Newark "Holy Stones": Context for Controversy,* Public symposium, Coshocton, Ohio, 1999.

#2. Squires, *Ancient Monuments of the Mississippi Valley,* 1847.

#3. Smith, *View of the Hebrews 1825,* Poultney, Vt. 1825.

#4. Berkley, [Blackett & Wilson], *The King Arthur Conspiracy,* Trafford Publishing, Canada, 2005.

#5. Michael, *Ancient Kentucke Inscriptions,* Chicago Spectrum Press, 2004.

#6. Berkley, [Blackett & Wilson], *Moses in the Hieroglyphs,* Trafford Publishing, 2006.

Ancient Kentucke Historical
Association Founders

/|\

Co-Founders

Barry Adams Rph

James Bland MD

Kenneth De Simone MD

James B. Michael*

Wallace Thompson*

David Withrow*

*Deceased

Ancient Kentucke Historical Association
2006-2007 Officers

President
James B. Michael
Ancient Kentucke Historian
Co-Founder

Vice President
Kenneth J. S. De Simone MD
Co-Founder

Treasurer
Thomas Clark DMD

Secretary
Marilyn Michael

Director-Film Production
Lee Pennington PHD

Director-Liaison
Adrienne Hardesty

Director-Research
Joseph Russell Adams

Advisor-Native America
Loren Jeffries

Ancient Kentucke Historical Association
/ | \
Membership

Membership dues in Ancient Kentucke Historical Association are $10 annually and include our monthly newsletter. Non-members are welcome to attend our meetings which are held twice each month in most months in the Kentuckiana area.

Our first book, **Ancient Kentucke Inscriptions Prince Madoc: Fact or Fiction,** sells for $25 American and includes USA postage

Checks for the above should be sent to:
Ancient Kentucke Historical Association
1324 Garden Hill Place
Louisville, Kentucky 40245

Email address:
marmakha@hotmail.com

Phone (502) 254-2414

ABOUT THE AUTHOR:

Degrees: University of Iowa, 1955, General Science, Pre-med.

Minor Degrees: Education, Psychology.

Advanced Work: Counseling and Guidance, Anthropology/ Archaeology at U of L, U of KY, Western KY Univ., Eastern KY Univ., Spalding Univ., (all in Kentucky)

Military: 44 years National Guard and Reserve. Assistant Battalion Surgeon, Medical evacuation pilot, Master Aviator, Ambulance Company Commander, Aviation Company Commander, Assistant Flight Operations Officer for the 103rd Division, Flight Operations Officer for the 102nd Division.

Work Experience: 32 years with Pfizer Pharmaceuticals: Sales Representative, Psychiatric Specialty Representative, and District Hospital Manager.

Offices Held:

Registrar: State of Kentucky for Sons of American Revolution.

President of Bacchus organization of Louisville, KY.

President of Leprechauns Senior Group of St. Patrick Church.

President of Ancient Kentucke Historical Association.

Appointment:

Ancient Kentucke Historian.

Visiting professorship:

Lagrange College, Hannibal, Missouri.

Gifted senior program at Central High School, Bullitt County, KY. for 10 years.

Gifted Student Program at St Patrick School, Louisville, KY.

Presentations:

Institute for Study of American Culture, Columbus, Georgia.

Sons of American Revolution, Louisville, Kentucky.

National Convention of Daughters of American Revolution, Louisville Kentucky.

BBC Radio, Cardiff, Wales, United Kingdom.

U.S. Native American Society, Hialeah, Florida.

Ancient American Artifacts Preservation Foundation, Michigan.

Over 175 presentations to historical organizations, Rotary, Kiwanis, and church groups in Kentucky, Indiana, Pennsylvania, Illinois, Florida, Michigan, and Massachusetts.

Index

A

B

C

D

DNA, 2, 6, 7, 68, 69, 70, 71, 72, 73, 74.
Druid, 4, 25, 76, 78, 779.

E

Earth mother-father, 64.
Easter Island, 6, 71.
Egyptian, hieroglyphics, 17, 22, 45, 93, 94.
Elucidator, 25, 26.
English, 4, 5, 29, 36, 47, 67, 84, 91, 93.
Etowah Mounds, 33.
Etruscan, 18.
Ezekiel, 25, 48, 64.

F

Fawn Hoof, 14, 20.
Fertile Crescent, 55.
Festival of Lights, 83.
Fort Ancient, 10.
Filson Club, 10, 11, 76.
Fischell, Dr., 88.

G

Gnostic, 35, 36, 66, 78, 79, 81, 92.
Greek, 15, 17, 18, 65, 70, 79.
Greek Orthodox, 79.

H

Haplogene, 7, 70.
Hanukkah, 77, 84.
Hawaii, 6, 69.
Heretics, 81, 82, 83.
Hermes, 65.
Helena, mother of Constantine, 79.
Hitler, 50, 56.
Hippo, council of, 80.

Holy Ghost, 51, 64.
Hopkins, Johns, 16, 17.

I

Iberia, 19.
Ice corridor, 6, 68.
Indianapolis, 23.
Indus Valley, 55,

J

Jansen, Dr. Donald, 1.
Jefferson, Pres. Thomas, 10.
Jeffries, Loren, 54, 96.
Jesus, 76, 78, 80, 91, 92.
Josephus, Flavius, 16.
Judah, 25.
Judas, gospel of, 82, 85.
Judea, tribe of, 79.

K

Kennewick Man, 6, 70.
Kentucky River, 14, 18.
Keystone, 88.
Khumric, 25, 53, 91, 92, 93.

L

Lene Lanape, 22, 25.
Leo, 45.
Leper, Dr. Bradley, 89, 90.
Levites, 79.
Lilly, Eli, 24, 25, 29.
Llandiff Cathedral, 35, 42, 43.
Lot's cave, 14.
Louisville, Kentucky, 10, 11, 45, 48, 76, 90.
Luke, Saint, 80.

M

Madoc, Prince, 1, 2, 3, 13, 43, 49, 76.
Magdalene, Mary, 72.
Mahan, Dr. Joseph, 51, 56.
Marcilinus, Armianas, 18.
McCulloch, Dr. Houston, 89, 91, 92.
Mediterranean, 33, 45, 52.
Meurig, King, 43.
Merrick, Rev., 88.
Mesopotamia, 14, 33, 41, 45, 48, 78.
Michael, Jim, 4, 13, 16, 21, 35, 38, 45, 48, 49, 50, 69, 70, 71, 72, 73, 74, 77,90, 94.
Mitchell, Dr. Samuel, 75.
Moses, 4, 91, 92, 93, 94.
Moundville Georgia, 33.

N

Nag Hammadi, 61, 80, 85.
Navaho, 54, 63, 65, 66, 67, 70.
Nazi, 50.
Nebuchadnezzar, 79, 94.
Newark Earthwork, 5, 83, 86, 87, 88, 90, 94.
Nicene Council, 78.

O

Ohio, 2, 5, 7, 9, 10, 11, 14, 73, 74, 85, 86, 87, 89, 94.
Orion, 45.
Ovate, 4.
Oxford, 76, 93.

P

Patrick, Saint, 48.
Paul, Pope II, 44.
Pen Dragon, Uthur, 43.

Pennington, Dr. Lee, 53, 54, 96.
Philadelphia, 28.
Philip, gospel of, 80.
Phrygia, 18.
Piankashaw, 8, 23.
Pittsburg, Pennsylvania, 7.
Polaris, 45, 47.
Popular Mechanics, 17.
Portsmouth, Kentucky, 10.
Powell, Dr. Mary, 39.
Priest, Josiah, 75, 77.

R

Rhaetian, 18.
Roman Catholic, 18, 35, 78, 79.

S

Saint Louis, 8.
Sanskrit, 55, 56.
Scotland, 75.
Scythian, 76.
Secret, The, 51, 56.
Serpens, 80, 81.
Serpent, 36, 38, 80.
Shanks, Hershel, 21.
Shawnee, 8, 9, 71.
Shishack, 16.
Siberia, 7, 70.
Sioux City, Iowa, 50.
Slade, Brian, 35, 36, 38.
Smith, Joseph, 73, 75.
Smithsonian, 68, 70, 85.
Solstice marker, 4, 14.
Solutrean, 6, 68.

Spirit Cave Man, 70.
Swastika, 33, 50, 51, 52, 53, 54, 55, 56, 58.

T

Tahiti, 6, 69.
Taurus, 45.
Ten Commandments, 85, 91.
Ten Lost Tribes of Israel, 5, 85, 91.
The Secret, 51, 56.
Thomas, Saint, 51, 80, 82.
Tin Island, 42, 52.
Tobacco, Chief, 8.
Transylvania, College, 14, 28.
Triune Vessel, 30.
Troy, 5, 35, 42, 52.
Turkey-track, 4.
Tuthmosis III, 16.

U

University of Kentucky, 4, 11, 14, 30, 39, 40.
Ur, 18, 33, 53, 55.

V

Vatican, 43, 45.
Velum, 25, 27.

W

Walam Olam, The, 22, 25, 28, 29.
Ward, Dr., 22, 24.
Warrior's Path, 9.
Webb, William, 3, 4, 11, 39, 44.
Welsh Dragon, 40, 41.
West Virginia, 69, 72.
White Water region, 22.
Williams, John, 70.

Wilson, Alan, 4, 14, 18, 20, 36, 45, 47, 53, 89, 90, 93, 94.
Winchester, Kentucky, 14.
Wyrick, David, 87, 88, 89, 90.

Y

Yahweh, 4, 5, 36, 38, 65.
Yuchi, 50, 56.